· *Oxford Scientific Films* ·

# OCEAN WILDLIFE

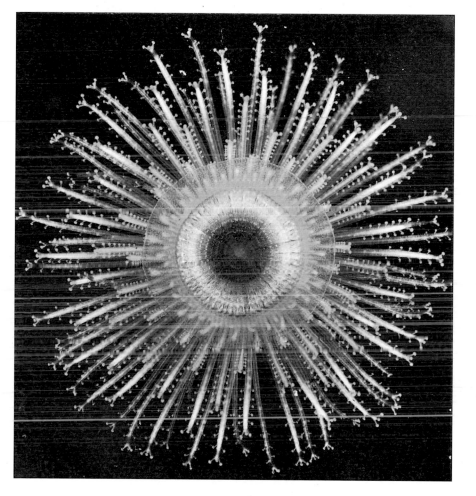

## *Martin Banks*

**MALLARD**
PRESS

MALLARD PRESS
An Imprint of BDD Promotional Book Company, Inc.,
666 Fifth Avenue, New York, NY 10103.

Mallard Press and its accompanying design and logo
are trademarks of BDD Promotional Book Company, Inc.

CLB 2338
Copyright © 1989 Colour Library Books Ltd.
© 1989 Illustrations: Oxford Scientific Films Ltd,
Long Hanborough, England.
Color separation by Hong Kong Graphic Arts Ltd, Hong Kong.
First published in the United States of America
in 1989 by The Mallard Press.
Printed and bound in Italy by Fratelli Spada, SpA.
ISBN 0 792 45026 4

# Contents

*These pages: a loggerhead turtle swims in the clear waters off Australia's Great Barrier Reef.*

*Previous page: a common blue jellyfish displays the symmetry and beauty of a snowflake.*

*1*
# The Vast Waters

Throughout history man has come into contact with the oceans, the vast areas of saltwater that cover over two-thirds of the total surface of the earth. Yet despite the fact that we have used the seas to transport us from one land mass to another, have harvested them for food and derived vital *minerals* like salt from them, we are only now beginning to learn very much about them.

Oceans reach great, sometimes incredible, depths. The floor of the ocean, like the surface of the land, *undulates* in a series of valleys and ridges. Neither flat nor even, half of the ocean floor is 11,000 feet below the surface. But there are much greater depths. In ocean trenches – chasms which bisect the ocean floor – the depth may reach 33,000 feet. Deepest of all is the Mariana Trench off South East Asia, which is 3,000 feet deeper than Mount Everest is high! And the ocean floor has its own "mountain" ranges, some of them higher than the highest mountains on land.

Oceans cover nearly seventy percent of the earth's surface and contain 5,500 million tons of sea water. While sea levels rise and fall through the ages, the actual volume of water contained in the oceans has remained remarkably constant throughout *geological* time. Oceans had their beginnings in the release of gases inside the newly-forming earth, which resulted in volcanic explosions that produced quantities of steam, rock and lava. As the planet began to cool, the steam condensed to water. This was made salty by minerals that drained off the land and into the rivers, which fed into the seas.

The seas which cover so much of the earth are all joined together. Paddle in the water in one spot and you are linked directly to almost all other seas around the world. We sub-divide

*Oceans cover seventy percent of the earth's total surface area.*

*Above: something of the mystery of the oceans is glimpsed in the strange "flight" of the manta ray.*

*Left: although the sea is its home, the whale must surface to breathe.*

this vast body of water using the natural divisions created by the larger continental land masses. The larger expanses of water we call oceans, the small ones, some of which are entirely landlocked, we call seas.

All over the earth's surface, sea water is constantly moving. The undulations on the surface are called waves. Waves are caused by the action of wind, which also plays an important part in the much larger-scale movement of water called currents. These are caused by a combination of wind direction, the earth's rotation and the shape of the continents. So ocean currents, which occur at all levels from the surface to the deeps, flow in a variety of directions and at a variety of speeds.

# 2
# Survival in the Ocean

Animal life began in the oceans. As many as ten million *species* of *organisms* may have existed in them since they were formed. Even today, the seas contain at least 160,000 species of animals, almost double the number that live on land, excluding insects.

Most of these creatures are truly marine. They can feed, breathe and reproduce without leaving the water at all. A myriad fishes, crabs, cuttlefish, *mollusks*, worms, sea urchins, and starfish make up the bulk of the marine animal community. Tiny, shrimp-like plankton abound in polar waters and provide food for other, larger marine animals, while corals inhabit the shallow waters of warm tropical seas.

Some species which now live in the oceans began life as land animals. Turtles are reptiles similar in appearance to the tortoises that live on land. They developed strong flippers instead of feet to aid their swimming. But despite this adaptation to an existence in water, the females still come ashore to lay their eggs, which need the sun's heat to incubate them. Penguins are examples of birds that have evolved an *aquatic* lifestyle, losing the power of flight as their wings became strong, paddle-like flippers to propel them through the water. Layers of blubber under the skin and a covering of tight, waterproof feathers help penguins and other seabirds to keep warm in the water, but they still need to come ashore to breed.

Large mammals have also evolved to spend their lives in the sea. Seals and sealions inhabit rocky shores and coasts in many parts of the world. They are fast and efficient swimmers, preying on fish which they catch underwater. But they haven't completely lost their dependence on the land either, for they need to come ashore to rest and breed. Whales and dolphins have forsaken land completely. These mammals, called cetaceans, live underwater and only come to the surface to breathe. Even their young are born in the sea. Cetaceans have streamlined bodies, and flippers and fins in place of legs to make them highly efficient swimmers. Living completely in the sea has allowed some whale species to grow to an enormous size, making them the largest of all living animals.

---

*Facing page top: a New Zealand fur seal displays its underwater acrobatic prowess.*

*Facing page bottom: having lost their power of flight, penguins have evolved to become expert swimmers.*

*Below: the streamlined body of a spotted dolphin makes this marine mammal a highly efficient swimmer.*

*3*

# Above the Oceans

Although the oceans themselves contain a wealth of animal life, the skies above the waves have their own animal inhabitants, too. Although only the birds possess a true ability to fly, some other creatures also seem to fly above the seas.

If you visit the beach, you will probably notice the seagulls, terns and wading birds which rely on the sea or the shoreline for their food. But many other birds live further out at sea, sometimes staying out of sight of land for many months at a time. The largest of these ocean-going birds are the albatrosses, huge gull-like birds that rank among the finest fliers in the world. They are masterful gliders, soaring effortlessly on steady wings. The largest species, the wandering albatross, has a wingspan of almost twelve feet. Albatrosses glide on stiff wings, obtaining their lift from winds deflected by the waves. This energy-saving method of flight allows albatrosses to make journeys of hundreds, even thousands of miles across the sea. Yet it also means they are unable to cross the windless calms of the tropics around the equator, so they remain in the southern hemisphere where they evolved.

Other birds, such as long-winged frigate birds,

*Above: a bottle-nosed dolphin leaping above the surface of the water.*

*Facing page: the gray-headed albatross ranks among the world's most spectacular gliders*

boobies and gannets, are expert at both flying and fishing, folding their wings and plunging from a great height into the waves to catch a fish, which they bring to the surface to swallow.

Much smaller petrels and shearwaters are found over all the oceans. They feed on small fish, squid and plankton, fluttering above the ocean swell and dipping down onto the waves to rest and feed.

But birds are not the only creatures to be seen above the oceans. In tropical waters there live several species of flying fish. They have fins which are elongated and allow them to glide 300 feet or more at a time above the water, though this is not true flight. "Flying" fish probably use this ability to escape from underwater *predators* .

Small cetaceans, like dolphins and porpoises, also jump clear of the water when they are traveling close to the surface. Propelling themselves forward at high speed, they leap above the surface in a series of graceful arcs. It's not done for fun, but as a way of saving energy, for the dolphin has to work harder to swim through the water than it does to travel through the air.

*A juvenile flying fish in the waters off Bermuda.*

# *4*
# The Edge of the Land

The floor of the ocean lies at varying depths beneath the sea, and different animals live at each of these levels. Where the sea meets the land, there is commonly a *zone* of shallow water, 300 feet deep, which may extend a mile or more out from shore. This is called a continental shelf and is caused by part of the land mass extending underneath the sea. Further out, the ocean bed shelves steeply to much greater depths.

These shallow waters contain a rich variety of animals and plants. If you visit the shore, you will often notice that when the tide goes out, the area of beach left exposed is covered with seaweed and shells which have been washed ashore. Where the shore is rocky, pools of seawater will be left among the rocks at low tide. If you look carefully, you can often find

*Bottom: a shore crab displays its fearsome claws.*

*Below: starfish are often to be seen along coasts between the high and low tide lines.*

*A sea otter feeds amid the kelp beds of California.*

many small animal inhabitants, like crabs, limpets, sea anemones, shrimps and even small fish, living in them. At high tide, when the sea covers the rocks, all these creatures move about quite freely again until some of them become trapped in rock pools at the next low tide.

The seaweeds which grow on rocky sea beds and shores provide food and shelter for many marine animals. Their waving fronds trap tiny organisms called *detritus* on which larger animals feed. There is a whole range of different seaweeds. Among the very smallest are algae, which coat the rocks, making them green and slippery to walk on at low tide. Viewed under water, the algae have tiny, frond-like projections. In some species, like sea lettuce, these fronds are like leaves. The largest seaweeds are called kelp. Kelp are the giants of underwater plant life, some varieties reaching up to ninety feet in length. They grow along rocky shores in a jumbled mat of floating leaves and stems that are rooted in the sea bed. A thick bed of kelp looks like an underwater forest.

*Sea anemones belong to the same group as jellyfish and coral.*

Kelp reduces the force of the waves and provides shelter for the many fish species that swim among the dense fronds. Off the western coast of North America, a strange mammal called the sea otter lives almost entirely in the kelp beds. From its floating home, the otter dives to catch clams and sea urchins. Sea urchins, spiny *invertebrates* called echinoderms, feed on the kelp. Without the sea otters, the kelp beds would eventually be destroyed by the sea urchins.

# 5
# Shifting Sands

Where the shallow floor of the ocean is sandy or muddy, a variety of burrowing creatures live on or below the sea bed. Mussels, clams and other shellfish which are encased in hard protective shell are called mollusks. Some have flat or streamlined shells to help them dig down through the sand. They also have a muscular foot which actually does the digging. Buried in the sand, mollusks feed by extending a pair of siphons to suck in food particles either lying at the surface or floating in the water. This is called filter feeding.

Other inhabitants of the sandy sea floor are bristle worms or polychaetes. They live in tubes or burrows. Tube worms construct their dwellings from grains of sand, bits of shell and spine, all glued together to create a fine, smooth finish. From its home, the tube worm extends feathery arms to catch food particles at the surface.

Lugworms live in U-shaped burrows. They feed by swallowing grains of sand and digesting the organic material that surrounds the grains. The used sand particles are then expelled to form piles of tubular castings at the entrance of the burrows. You can often find them on mudflats at low tide.

*Echinoderms* such as starfish, sea urchins and sea cucumbers burrow into the sandy sea floor, too. So do hermit crabs, which come out to scavenge for food. All these creatures live in burrows to avoid being swept away by the constant motion of currents and waves.

The shifting sands give little hold for seaweeds, which are much more common where the sea bed is rocky. But in sheltered, shallow waters, seagrasses grow instead. The commonest ones, called zostera, are fine and pale green. Tiny seahorses and other pipefish shelter and swim among these underwater meadows, the seahorses holding onto the waving grass blades with their prehensile tails.

Larger fish species also inhabit this sandy

sea floor. The strange-looking flatfish have become specially designed for living on the sea bed. The body of a flatfish is flattened to allow it to rest on the sea floor. The fish is actually lying on its side, but its head has changed position and its eyes are situated on top of its skull so that it can watch the water above for food or danger. Flatfish always remain on, or close to, the seabed. They are camouflaged with a mottled or spotted skin, and can even change color according to whether they are resting on pale sand or much darker gravel.

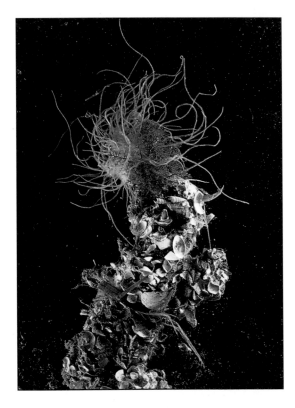

*Above: a tube worm "Loimia medusa" in its protective tube constructed of grains of sand and broken shell.*

*Facing page top: pipefish shelter and swim among underwater meadows of seaweed.*

*Facing page bottom: a flounder lies well camouflaged against the sand of the sea bed.*

# 6
# Creatures
# of the Coral

Most colorful of all the ocean's *habitats* is the coral reef. Corals are living animals, usually found in large colonies, and are responsible for the largest structures made by any animal on earth. A coral consists of a tiny *polyp*, an anemone-like creature, which provides a chalky skeleton outside its body. Over millions of years, the *exoskeletons* of these tiny creatures build together into a coral formation.

*Above: a diagonal-lined butterfly fish in the waters of the Red Sea.*

*Left: a shoal of brightly colored sea gold fish swim among the coral formations of the Red Sea.*

Coral grows fastest in shallow tropical waters where there is plenty of sunlight. This encourages algae to grow among the coral polyps, producing the limestone which is required to bond the calcium deposits together to form a coral growth. Corals occur in many shapes and sizes. The same species may produce slender fans or branches in calm waters, but thicker, more rounded shapes in heavy surf. Mollusk shells and worm tubes also add to the growth of the coral mass.

Coral are member of the *coelenterates*, a group which also contains sea anemones and

*Above: a clown fish swims among the anemones of the Great Barrier Reef.*

*Left: a beautifully colored tube sponge.*

---

the sea fans and red corals, called soft corals. Coral beds also contain many thick-shelled mollusks, including the huge giant clam, three to four feet across and avoided by divers because of its ability to snap shut on a man's leg and hold him fast.

Many of the coral dwellers match the splendor of their home. Octopuses live in caves and crannies, changing colour to match their brilliant surroundings. Shoals of strangely-marked fish dart among the coral formations, their vivid colors providing an effective *camouflage*. Some coral-dwelling fish have

evolved special feeding methods. The angel and butterfly fish have long snouts and sharp teeth to reach into crevices in the coral for food. The teeth of the parrot fish are fused together like a beak to chip off pieces of coral to eat. Some species are equipped with poisonous spines to warn off predators, while others take refuge in the coral itself to escape danger.

As coral organisms live in the sea, vertical growth of the coral depends on the sea level. Over the last 100,000 years the sea level has been rising, allowing coral to grow at up to half an inch per year in an upwards direction. At the same time, some reefs are threatened with destruction by one creature, the crown-of-thorns starfish. In the Pacific Ocean, this species is multiplying very rapidly, and because the starfish feeds on the coral-making organisms, less new coral is being constructed, and some reefs are being *eroded*.

7
# Floating on the Ocean

*The Portuguese man-of-war drifts about tropical waters buoyed by its air sack and carried by the action of wind and current.*

Some animals live on the surface of the sea. Chief among them are the siphonophores, which, though they look like large jellyfish, belong to a class of animals called hydrozoa. Best known is the Portuguese man-of-war, usually found far out at sea in warm tropical waters, drifting at the surface and exposed to the waves, wind and sun.

Like sea urchins and sea anemones, the man-of-war is a coelenterate. It lacks a heart, a skeleton, brain and the complex digestive and nervous systems found in more highly-developed animals. It is actually formed of many tiny polyps – simple creatures living together in a colony which is comprised of several different parts called persons.

At the surface, the animal has a large, gas-filled, transparent bag or float, which is surmounted by a crest used as a sail. Below the surface, long, curled tentacles from nine to ninety feet in length trail down into the water. There are also stomach and reproductive persons which play their own parts in supporting the colony.

A Portuguese man-of-war is carried along by the action of wind and current. The sail may occur either to the left or right side of the float, so the wind blows some of the animals in one direction, and the others the opposite way. This allows them to be more evenly dispersed over the oceans.

Because the waters nearest to the surface are the richest in plankton, small fish and shrimps concentrate here to feed. These are the main food of the man-of-war, which drifts along trawling its tentacles through the water. Fully extended, the hair-like tentacles may be seventy times longer than when they are coiled. If a small animal brushes against a tentacle, the nearest *nematocysts* react by shooting sharp threads into the prey, injecting it with poison. This paralyzes the animal, which is then hauled up to be eaten by the stomach persons.

Another surface dweller is a small snail, which is one of the man-of-war's principal enemies. The bubble raft snail creates its own raft made of air bubbles trapped from the surface in a slimy mucus produced by its foot. On its raft of bubbles, the snail rides across the sea, readily feeding on the Portuguese man-of-war, to whose poisonous tentacles it is apparently immune.

*Facing page top: just over an inch in length, this sea slug has a delicate, flower-like appearance.*

*Facing page bottom: the bubble raft snail preys upon jellyfish. It is seen here feeding on a Jack sail-by-wind.*

*8*

# Plankton and its Grazers

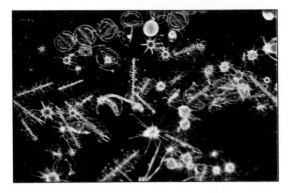

*Plankton forms the basis of the oceanic food chain.*

Plankton consists of tiny plants and animals which drift in suspension close to the surface of the oceans. It forms a valuable food on which a great variety of other oceanic animals feed. Plankton consists of two types: phytoplankton and zooplankton. Phytoplankton is made up of single-celled plants and algae.

Close to the surface, phytoplankton forms a drifting pasture of high protein food which the smaller zooplankton feeds on. Zooplankton consists of a great many different species of small marine animals. Plankton grows and develops at its greatest rate in the upper 200 feet of the ocean. This is called the sunlit zone, and sunlight encourages the development of plankton, which grows fastest at depths of between five-and-a-half and eight feet. Plankton is most abundant where the sea is rich in *nutrients*, particularly nitrates and phosphates. Phytoplankton achieves its greatest development in the cold polar seas where, in spring and early summer, increases in daylight and higher temperatures cause it to "bloom" in sudden abundance and then die off again as it uses up the available nutrients.

Zooplankton consists of many groups of animals, principally protozoas, ciliates, coelenterates and tiny crustaceans. These are eaten by slightly larger species, including minute fish and a number of shrimp-like species, one commonly called krill. Krill is particularly abundant in Antarctic waters, where it forms about ninety percent of the zooplankton. In other oceans, many of the animals which make up the zooplankton mass are the young or larval stages of other marine species.

The zooplankton forms the main food source for a wide variety of much larger ocean dwellers, including fish such as herring, mackerel and flying fish, a variety of bird species and even the basking and whale sharks, which feed close to the surface where plankton is the most abundant.

Several species of whales feed chiefly on plankton too. These huge mammals have enormous mouths, and in the Antarctic they take in gallons of krill-rich seawater at a single draught. Baleen plates in the sides of the mouth sieve the water and the whale swallows the krill. A large baleen whale will devour several tons of krill in the course of a day's feeding.

Plankton is the basis of the oceanic *food chain*. These tiny organisms represent the richest and most abundant food supply the oceans produce.

*Above: the young of the squid are one of the many species that go to make up the zooplankton mass.*

*Facing page: viewed through a microscope, plankton reveals its surprising beauty.*

*9*

# Predators of the Sea

At the opposite end of the food chain from the plankton are marine predators, animals which hunt and feed on other, smaller creatures. Best known are the sharks, which have a skeleton made of cartilage, not bone, and which lack a swim bladder, which in other fish helps to keep them afloat.

There are over 300 different species of sharks. They have a streamlined body shape to allow fast swimming and turning when in pursuit of their prey, usually fish and squid. Sharks have poor eyesight, but they can detect food with their very acute sense of smell. Sharks also possess a lateral line system, a series of sensory receptors which can detect the tiny electronic impulses made by fish and other prey moving through the water.

Sharks have a reputation as man-eaters. In fact, very few species have ever been known to attack people. Those that sometimes do belong to a group called requiem sharks, including the most feared of all, the great white shark. Great whites, like most sharks, are usually restricted to warmer waters, where they prey extensively on seals and sealions. Almost every attack on people by these sharks is the result of the swimmer being mistaken for their natural prey.

Sharks are not the only predatory fish that live in the oceans. Tropical waters are also the home of the barracuda. This powerful-bodied fish has jaws armed with sharp teeth. Barracudas feed on other fish, charging into the shoals and snatching their quarry with bites of lightning speed. In places like the West Indies, barracudas are feared as much as sharks, in the belief that they attack people deliberately. However, it seems that barracudas, too, only attack people whom they mistake for their natural prey.

Other predators that live in warm tropical seas include moray eels and octopuses, which lie in wait for prey in the shelter of crevices or caves in underwater rock or coral formations. The moray eel pounces on fish, which it grabs and bites with its long, sharp teeth. Octopuses,

*Top: a shoal of chevron barracuda; powerful predators of tropical waters.*

*Above: an olive sea snake.*

*Facing page top: the fearsome moray eel is an inhabitant of warm, shallow waters.*

*Facing page bottom: a gray reef shark, one of over 300 different species of this most feared marine predator.*

with their long, suckered tentacles and beak-like mouths are more slow moving. They feed extensively on crabs, breaking open the shells with their powerful jaws.

The largest mammal predator in the sea is the killer whale, which lives in groups of about twenty or more individuals and is distributed over all the world's oceans. The killer whale is a fast swimmer, using its very sharp teeth and powerful bite to prey on fish, seabirds, seals and even other smaller cetaceans like dolphins.

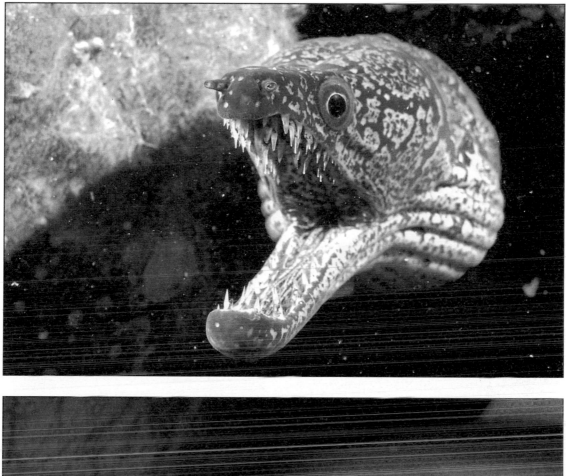

## 10
# Fish Shoals

The surface waters of the oceans are inhabited by many species of fish. The smaller species are attracted to feed on the plankton which grow rapidly wherever upwelling currents carry nutrients from the ocean floor. Many species of plankton undertake a daily *migration*, moving further down below the surface during the daytime, and returning upwards toward the surface at night. The plankton feeders follow them into this darker twilight zone, called the dysphotic zone, between 150 and 300 feet below the surface. Many of the fish species of the sunlit and dysphotic zones, like herring, anchovies and sardines, live in gatherings called shoals. They are protectively colored, having dark backs and pale or silvery underparts. This helps them

*Left: a shoal of sardines. Living in large groups gives many smaller fish a kind of protection.*

*Above: many fish have shiny, flashing scales that mirror their surroundings and confuse predators.*

to blend with their surroundings and to escape from attack either from the surface, or from below. If seen from above, the fish blend with the darker waters below, while predators approaching them from the twilight zone can be confused by their shiny, flashing underparts, which mirror the surroundings.

Living in large shoals gives smaller fish a sort of safety in numbers, since it is often more difficult for a predator to single out and catch

*A shoal of Almaco Jacks feeding on fry.*

one fish among a crowd of hundreds zig-zagging through the water. The smaller fish species, like herring, feed on plankton in their earlier stages but, as they grow, move to other food items, such as crustaceans. Finally, when adult, sand eels and tiny fish form their main diet.

There are other predatory fish in the open ocean. Among the smallest is the mackerel, which feeds on smaller, plankton-eating fish. Mackerel have a streamlined shape and a strong, forked tail, and the upper and lower portions of their bodies are differently colored. They are the smaller relatives of some of the fastest-swimming fish in the seas, like tuna, which may may reach over twelve feet in length and weigh up to 1,800 lbs, and the strange-looking swordfish

with its long, thin, elongated snout. They normally live in tropical oceans, though swordfish sometimes enter colder waters too. Among the fastest swimmers of all are the sailfish and marlin. These big fish are called game fish, for they are favorite prizes for sport-fishermen because of their great size and strength.

More importantly for man, the open waters of the oceans harbor a great marine harvest in the fish which inhabit the upper zones. Over 75 million tons of fish are harvested each year from the world's oceans.

## *11*
# Mysterious Migrations

Some oceanic animals undertake long journeys or migrations. Many of the baleen whales travel hundreds of miles each year between their feeding grounds in the plankton-rich seas around the North and South Poles, and their breeding grounds in the warm water of the tropics. Each species uses its own feeding and wintering grounds. Some, like humpback, gray and right whales, have separate populations living in each *hemisphere*. Because the seasons are the opposite in each hemisphere, one population is feeding in polar waters while the other is giving birth to its young in tropical waters.

Just how whales make journeys to exactly the same waters hundreds of miles apart every spring and autumn remains a mystery. Possibly they use the appearance of the ocean floor to guide them like a map, or even the positions of the moon, stars and sun as a means of navigation.

The migration of eels is even more mysterious. Eels spend most of their lives in fresh water lakes and rivers, but they are born in the sea and return there as adults to breed. For centuries, very tiny eels were never found and consequently nobody understood where they came from. Finally, biologists proved that a small, flattened-looking fish was actually the very early stage of the baby eel, which later transformed into the familiar, long-bodied shape as it grew up. In their earliest stages, European and American eels are only found in one place: the Sargasso Sea in the southwest Atlantic. This is an area of calm water covered in dense sargassum weed (which harbors the plankton on which the eels first feed) and surrounded by strong currents. From here, young eels are carried by the currents to the coasts of America and Europe. European eels take three years to arrive, by which time they already look like eels and are known as elvers. They travel up rivers, where they grow to maturity. Much later, eels in

---

*A minke whale feeding in the plankton-rich seas of Antarctica.*

breeding condition make the return journey of over 600 miles to the Sargasso Sea to start another generation.

Salmon make long migrations in the opposite direction. They are born in fresh water, where they remain feeding and growing for the first three years of their lives. Salmon of several different species live in both Pacific and Atlantic oceans, all of them making similar journeys back to the rivers of their birth when they are ready to lay their eggs or *spawn*. Finding their way is an amazing feat of underwater navigation that, like the journeys of the great whales, still remains largely unexplained.

*Right: Sargassum weed harbors the plankton upon which eels first feed.*

*Below: originating in the Sargasso Sea, elvers (young eels) are carried by ocean currents to the coasts of America and Europe.*

## *12*
# Darkest Depths

Descend deep down into the oceans, and the waters become darker as the sunlight ceases to penetrate. One hundred and fifty feet below the surface, light is already dimmed as you enter the twilight zone. Most of the predatory fish, including many species of sharks, are found here. Below 1,800 feet there is no sunlight at all, and the water temperature is much lower. The animals that live in this cold, dark world have adapted to the lack of light and the increased pressure.

At these depths, food is much scarcer. Deep-sea animals have developed special methods for hunting prey. Most have poorly-developed eyes, for sight is of little value in the darkness. Some species are quite blind, having no eyes at all. Instead, the hunters are equipped with

*The deep sea angler fish has a lure attached to its mouth which it uses to attract prey.*

sensory devices for locating their prey, which allow them to detect changes in the water pressure caused by the movements of other animals. Some deep-sea fish have strange lumps and spikes on their bodies which serve this purpose. These fish often have cavernous mouths, lined with rows of fearsome teeth, designed to catch any food that comes within range. Many deep-sea animals, including fish, octopuses and squid, have organs called photopores on their bodies. These contain light-producing bacteria which illuminate the animals in the dark waters.

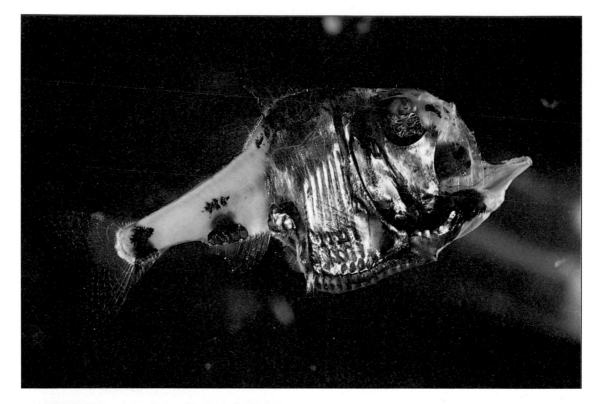

*Top: the deep sea hatchet fish is among the most grotesque of animals. On the lower edge of each side of its body (above) it possesses rows of photopores, or light-producing organs.*

The angler fish has a strange, branch-like growth on the top of its head which gives off this form of light. The fish uses it as a sort of fishing rod to attract prey within the reach of its huge mouth.

Few deep sea animals reach enormous size, though some large animals, like the deep-diving sperm whale and the giant squid, do exist. Typical species are limited in size by the small amounts of food that reach these depths from the richer levels above. For example, the strange-looking angler fishes, of which there are many species, rarely grow to more than a few inches in length.

The floor of the ocean deeps consists of thick *sediments*. In this ooze many animals manage to survive on bacteria living on its surface or in the water above. Worms and mollusks, related to similar species in shallow waters, are eaten by the ever-present echinoderms, particularly brittlestars, which scavenge in large numbers over the ooze in search of any suitable food items.

## 13
# Deep Sea Oases

Until recently, all life was thought to rely on sunlight to make food through the process called *photosynthesis*. Life at the bottom of the sea was thought to be possible only because of the sparse foods that reached these depths from the sunlit waters at the surface.

*Exploration of hydrothermal vents in the Pacific in the 1970s revealed the unexpected presence of whole communities of animals.*

In 1977 a startling new discovery was made about life in the deep oceans. Scientists already believed that in some of the deepest valleys in the ocean bed, underwater vents were created by the plates of the earth's crust moving slowly apart, allowing hot water and gases to escape into the ocean.

Scientists searched first in the Pacific Ocean, where parts of the sea floor are spreading apart relatively quickly. The first vents were found in the seas east of the Galapagos Islands, but no one was prepared for the discovery of whole animal communities surrounding them.

Using a specially-designed submersible craft that could pluck animals from the ocean floor, biologists discovered a range of animals new to science. Clusters of long, red worms live in tubes attached to the rocks and also in "chimneys" produced by sulphur deposits discharged from the vents. Anemones, clams, barnacles, leeches and bristleworms are all present in large numbers. Even a new siphonophore, related to the Portuguese man-of-war, but living at the bottom of the ocean instead of on the surface, was discovered.

Vents were later found at even greater depths in the Atlantic Ocean. Here clams and worms were almost absent, but free-swimming animals, like blind shrimps and eel-like fish, were abundant.

The discovery of these thriving underwater communities posed the question of how they manage to survive. The escaping hot water cools rapidly in the cold ocean, so that many species can live close to the vents without harm. The springs are also rich in sulphur, and sulphur compounds can support large numbers of bacteria. In their turn, the bacteria provide the nutrients forming the basis of the vent community food chain.

These undersea oases are the first evidence of animal life being able to support itself without deriving any energy, however indirectly, from the sun. They are proof, too, of how little we know about life in and under the sea. Despite the fact that the oceans cover so much of the earth's surface, they still harbor a great many secrets from us, and are likely to do so for long into the future.

# Glossary

**AQUATIC** Living only on or in the water, and not on the land.

**CAMOUFLAGE** The ability of an animal to use its color or shape to blend in with its surroundings.

**COELENTERATE** A jelly-like animal such as a jellyfish, sea anemone or coral. Coelenterate is Latin for "hollow gut".

**DETRITUS** Organic debris which is derived from decomposing debris and which forms food for other organisms.

**ECHINODERMS** Spiny-skinned animals, like starfish, sea cucumbers, urchins and brittlestars, all having their bodies arranged symmetrically around the mouth.

**EROSION** The gradual wearing away of a solid surface by the action of wind or water.

**EXOSKELETON** A skeleton covering the outside of the body, or situated in the skin.

**FOOD CHAIN** The relationship or network linking animals by the foods that they eat. In the oceans, plankton are at the bottom of the food chain, and sharks and killer whales are at the top.

**GEOLOGICAL** Relating to the age and nature of the earth's covering or crust. Geological time spans the period from the creation of the earth and continues to the present day.

**HABITAT** The natural home or type of surroundings in which an animal or plant is found.

**HEMISPHERE** The world is divided into two hemispheres, the northern and the southern, which are separated by the equator at the line of "0" degrees latitude.

**MIGRATION** A regular journey undertaken by animals, usually at certain seasons of the year, in order to find better food or improved climatic conditions.

**MINERAL** Any form of non-organic substance which is produced from the earth.

**NEMATOCYSTS** The stinging cells of coelenterate animals, usually located in the tentacles.

**NUTRIENTS** Substances which provide nourishment and promote growth in plants or animals.

**POLYP** A simple, tubular-shaped animal having a mouth at one end, and usually bearing tentacles – the most basically shaped coelenterate.

**PREDATOR** An animal that hunts other animals for food.

**SEDIMENT** Layers of fine mud or sand which lie on the ocean floor.

**SPAWNING** The mating and egg-laying process of fish.

**SPECIES** The term used to describe a particular type of animal and distinguish it from others.

**ZONE** An area or level which has clearly defined boundaries.